About the Future

By
Evangelist Dea Warford

As revealed in the
Book of Revelation

About The Future

Warford Ministries   www.deawarford.org

ISBN: 978-1-7352994-6-4

Edited by Linda Stephens and Norm Rush

Cover and Formatting by Shannon Herring www. ChristianEditingandDesign.com

Published by Warford Ministries
www.deawarford.org

Contents

Introduction

If I could tell you what is likely to happen in the near future, would you be interested in knowing?

The prophetic writings of St. John in the book of Revelation tells us a great deal **About the Future**. If you have never read Revelation, or haven't in a long time, read it! It is the companion study to the book now in your hands. If you doubt the Bible is true, keep an open mind. What if the billion plus Christians who believe it are right? Read the following descriptions of unfolding events broadcast on television news reports that were long ago already written in the Bible, inspired by the only one in the universe who knows what our future holds. Like it or not, our faces may be indelibly painted in those pictures! Get ready for a rollercoaster ride through tomorrow...

FASTEN YOUR SEATBELT!

1

Flying Saucers

"The stars fell from the sky to the earth" (Rev. 6:13).

Stars? From the sky? Falling to Earth? What could St. John have been describing? Consider this...

On June 24, 1947, Kenneth Arnold, a private pilot, was flying a small plane not far from Mount Rainier in Washington State when he noticed something unusual. Nine objects with a bluish hue shot across the sky, reflecting the Sun's rays in flashes. Arnold later reported they seemed to be maybe fifty feet wide. They were flying faster, by far, than any aircraft at the time. Unlike airplanes or jets, they changed direction abruptly.

After landing, Arnold told the airport staff about the unidentified objects. When news reporters interviewed him, the sighting was reported nationwide on TV, radio, and in newspapers. Because Arnold described the unknown flying objects as "saucers skipping across water," subsequent sightings were called "flying saucers." Soon, reports of many Unidentified Flying Objects (UFO's) came from around America. Such sightings continue even today.

Are UFO's real? There is too much evidence, and many witnesses who claim to have seen UFO's, to discount everything. UFOs can only be one of three things...

1. Aliens from another planet:

In 1976, I published an article in a local newspaper shortly before the USA Viking spacecraft was about to land on Mars (scientists were hoping to find evidence of life there). I wrote that no life would be found on Mars. And they did NOT find any evidence of life. Over the next four decades, all attempts by rocket scientists and astronomers to find evidence of life on other planets also failed.

The belief (or hope) of life on other planets is fed not by evidence but by science fiction writers and dreamers. If man evolved as biology now teaches, then humans are likely just one of many evolved species. There are 200 billion trillion stars, so many believe life surely must have also evolved on other planets surrounding other stars in the universe. And so, the search continues. But, even if beings were on other planets, they would have no salvation.

The Bible says God only had one Son, and He died to save the people of Earth: **"God sent his Son into the world** (not Mars or Endor), **not to condemn the world, but to save the world"** (John 3:17).

Only our World has a Savior to save us from our sins. Satan loves to diminish humanity's destiny as the center of the universe and the center of God's love, eternal affection, and attention. The theory of evolution (without God guiding it) and belief in aliens and life on other planets distract many from the most important and eternal truths.

2. Demons:

"Satan disguises himself as an angel of light" (2 Cor. 11:14). If Satan can masquerade as an angel, an army of demons could also be "disguised as aliens from another planet." Jude 13 likens evil men to,

"wandering stars for whom gloomy darkness is kept forever." Could these "stars" allude to "fallen angels" wandering in the heavens, awaiting judgment day? And are these fallen angels ("wandering stars") some of the UFO's occasionally reported? People who claim they were abducted by aliens are further evidence of demonic activity. Monstrous creatures take them into "spacecraft" and "examine" them as in "scientific" experiments. I am an exorcist and have cast demons out of more than one woman who felt beings come into her bedroom at night and "do things" (sexually) to her.

Genesis 6:2-4 describes fallen angels who became fascinated with women (and sex) and took upon themselves human bodies so they could sleep with them.

These were the angels described in Jude 6: **"He held angels for judgment on the great day. They were held in darkness, bound by eternal chains. These are the angels who didn't keep their position of authority but abandoned their assigned place."**

From this angelic and human "union" came a species of giants, "mighty men" (Gen. 6:4). This half-human race was destroyed in the worldwide flood of Noah's time. Are their bones the Neanderthal discovered by paleontologists?

If men today (and even some fallen preachers) sell their souls for a woman and sex, I don't find it hard to believe an angel could fall away from God for a woman! If this sounds fantastic, I submit it isn't half as fantastic as bug-eyed, giant-headed, green aliens flying around in saucers beaming up people to experiment on them! If UFOs aren't aliens or demons, then they could be...

3. Angels:

Angels are called stars in several places in Revelation:

"The seven stars are the angels of the seven churches" (Rev. 1:20 NKJV). If Jesus calls angels "stars," then UFO's appearing in the heavens, like stars flashing in the sky, could be angels. The Prophet Ezekiel mentions angels, and it sounds like he is describing what people mistakenly have called "flying saucers."

In Ezekiel 1:14-16, the prophet speaks of angels and "wheels." **"The living creatures ran back and forth like lightning. As I looked at the living creatures, I saw a wheel on the ground beside each of them. This is how the wheels looked and how they were made"**

What Ezekiel described as "wheels" could today be described as "saucers." Every Christmas, we hear of the wise men who ask: **"Where is the one who was born to be the king of the Jews? We saw his star rising and have come to worship him"** (Matt. 2:2).

The wise men were scientists, scholars, and priests from ancient nations of Persia and Arabia. We don't know how they knew a star rising in the east indicated the birth of the King of Israel. Perhaps an angel announced it to them, or some prophet had spoken of its coming. Yet they were so convinced of its truth they traveled a great distance from the Middle East to witness Christ's first coming.

Today, the Middle East has captured the attention of all nations. Their significant oil deposits, training and encouragement of terrorists, and Iran's seeking to develop atomic weapons are alarming! This could be further evidence these are the last days as men "from the (middle) east" are "announcing" Christ's Second Coming. The "star in the east" the wise men saw could hardly have been an actual star. Stars are up to millions of miles in diameter. Over a million Earths could fit in our Sun, a very average-sized star. Matt. 2:9 described the star as preceding the wise men until it "stood above" where the infant Jesus lay in a manger. A star could indicate the primary direction but not stand above an exact spot (It would incinerate everybody!). It must have been something else.

That Christmas "star" could have been but the first "unidentified flying object" reported so often since 1947. Are these "stars" (mistaken for alien aircraft) a sign like the "star in the east" the wise men saw hovering over the place of Christ's birth? And, just as the star announced the birth of Christ, could the UFO's be announcing Christ's soon return? Jesus warned that in the last days, there would be such things as:

"**...fearful sights and great signs shall there be from heaven**" (Luke 21:11). "**Miraculous signs will occur in the sun, moon, and stars**" (Luke 21:25). "**Immediately after the misery of those days, the sun will turn dark, the moon will not give light, the stars will fall from the sky, and the powers of the universe will be shaken**" (Matt. 24:29).

UFO's, looking like "stars," could be part of the fulfillment of these verses. Fantastic signs from heaven catching the world's attention will broadcast the end is near:

"When you see these things happen, you know that the kingdom of God is near. I can guarantee... This generation will not disappear until all this takes place" (Luke 21:31, 32).

Many alive today are still among the "generation" that has read about, watched movies about, and even seen UFO's. I have thought about it all my life. According to Jesus, this "generation" (the one on Earth as these "signs" are happening), though maybe elderly, will see the kingdom of God come. I conclude UFO's are both angels and demons.

When Christ's disciples asked Him about the last days, the first thing Jesus told them was, "Be careful that you are not deceived" (Luke 21:8). Demons appearing in the skies would love for people to think these UFO's are just aliens from another planet, thus focusing their minds on this deception. (Any angels appearing are not deceiving us but are the fulfillment of the "signs in the heavens" calling mankind to prepare for our final days on Earth). This is an exciting time!

In the next chapter, we'll study more about angels. Before we do, may I ask...

Are you ready for YOUR final days on Earth?

2

Angels

"The seven angels who had the seven trumpets got ready to blow them" (Rev. 8:6).

The book of Revelation is filled with descriptions of coming great calamities, wars, storms, famines, and plagues. Seven angels will announce these events by making a loud noise, likened to blasts from trumpets. The whole world will hear and see the unfolding of Revelation's prophetic events.

Angels are featured prominently in the closing days. In fact, they are mentioned 72 times in Revelation!

What are angels? They are created beings the Lord made before He created man or even the earth.

"You made him (man) **a little lower than the angels**» (Heb. 2:7 NKJV).

Angels are a superior race to humans. They are doubtless smarter and certainly stronger. Some angels are called "mighty" (Rev. 10:1). They are also spirits. He "makes His angels spirits" (Hebrews 1:7 NKJV).

So, angels do not have a physical body: **"a spirit does not have flesh and bones"** (Luke 24:39 NKJV).

Angels can fly as they are not bound to the earth by gravity. Most do NOT have wings. Not once does Revelation mention angels having wings. However, two classes of angels are described as having wings, Seraphim and Cherubim. They serve exceptional assignments, like surrounding the throne of God (Isaiah 6:1-3, Exodus 25:20). Painters and artists in the Middle Ages assumed all angels, like the Seraphim and Cherubim, had wings; thus wings were repeatedly painted on angels. This idea remains even today.

Angels frequently appeared to people in the Bible, and they were, at times, mistaken for men. If those angels had wings, don't you think those to whom they appeared would afterward comment of their wings, "Say, did you notice something unusual about those guys?"

We know there are at least 100,000,000 angels (Rev. 5:11). This was how many St. John was shown, but there could be billions more.

Since the beginning of man, angels have been busy on earth. Angels don't just stand around heaven, playing harps. Cherubim angels were sent to guard the tree of life when Adam and Eve were expelled from the Garden of Eden (Genesis 3:24). They have brought messages to mankind since Genesis 16:7,11, when an angel announced the birth of Ishmael. Two angels warned of God's judgment upon Sodom (19:1). They helped rescue Lot from judgment (19:15), fought wars for Israel (Ex. 33), encouraged a discouraged Gideon (Judges 6:12), and announced Samson's birth (Judges 13:3). I could go on and on. Angels are mentioned over 270 times in the Bible!

Angels figured prominently in the Christmas story 2,000 years ago. They are still celebrated in songs, decorations, and even topping Christmas trees. The angel Gabriel announced the birth of Christ to Mary (Luke 1:26-37). The angel of the Lord announced His birth to shepherds (Luke 2:9) and then to Joseph in a dream (Matt. 1:20); stories told over and over each holiday season.

Often on a spiritually significant day in biblical history, angels were mentioned as somehow involved, or we can certainly infer they were behind the scenes because angels help Christians by warning us (Matt. 2:19), encouraging us (Acts 27:23), and protecting us (Psalm 34:7, Ex. 23:20, 23, Isa. 63:9). That angels are involved in our lives shows God cares about us. He has chosen to remain invisible yet proves His love and concern for our welfare through other means.

One way, besides angels, God proves His love is by giving us His Word in print, the Bible.

"The Holy Scriptures...have the power to give you wisdom so that you can be saved through faith in Christ Jesus. Every Scripture passage is inspired by God. All of them are useful for teaching, pointing out errors, correcting people, and training them for a life that has God's approval" (2 Tim. 3:15, 16).

God also reveals Himself to us through men (for instance, preachers like me!)

"It pleased God by the foolishness of preaching to save them that believe" (1 Cor.1:21 KJV).

God demonstrates His vast power and intelligence through nature: **"What can be known about God is clear to them because he has made it clear to them. From the creation of the world, God's invisible qualities, his eternal power and divine nature, have been clearly observed in what he made. As a result, people have no excuse"** (Romans 1:19, 20).

God reveals Himself also through angels, especially at very needy times, and the last days will be VERY NEEDY times! After Jesus had fasted and prayed and battled with Satan for 40 days (Luke 4:2), God honored and comforted Him by sending angels to attend to His needs (Matthew 4:11). Then, as Christ wrestled in the garden with the impending agony of the cross (Luke 22:43), angels came to comfort and strengthened Him there as well.

Following is a true account of how angels appeared when needed the most.

Jim Elliot was an American missionary in the 1950s to the primitive Auca Indians of Ecuador. He had to fly by airplane to visit a Huaorani tribe with little exposure to the outside world. Tragically, before Jim and several other missionaries could share the gospel with the natives, they were all speared to death, even as they were lovingly trying to help them. The movie "End of the Spear" shares their story. What follows is a true account of how angels appeared when needed the most.

One of the Indians who personally speared Jim to death was later converted to Christ. He reported that as the Huaorani were martyring the Americans, the warriors and the dying men saw angels in heaven hovering over this tragic sight. And they could hear them singing! God had honored these mighty men of God at their untimely death by sending a choir of angels to sing them into eternity!

Hard times are coming soon to this planet as we will see in Revelation. Christians will need special grace to survive financially, physically, and spiritually. Some will surely face martyrdom like Jim Elliot and these other missionaries. Be assured even as the angels were there in the garden to strengthen Jesus and were in heaven, singing welcoming choruses to dying missionaries, angels can be there in your future when you need them the most!

We're on the brink of eternity. Revelation shows angels will be involved in the closing events of this age, including:

- Sounding trumpets announcing spectacular events coming to the planet (Ch. 9 and Cherubim as pictured at the start of this chapter)

- Pouring out terrible judgments on a Christ-rejecting world (Ch. 16)

- And, finally, casting Satan alive into Hell (Rev. 20:1).

One happy day all who believe will join the angels in the mightiest choir ever assembled (Rev. 5:11). It will make the Mormon Tabernacle Choir look like a mosquito solo! I don't want to miss it, do you? An angel appeared to shepherds in a field when,

"Suddenly, a large army of angels appeared with the angel. They were praising God by saying, 'Glory to God in the highest heaven, and on earth peace to those who have his good will!'" (Luke 2:1, 2).

Angels singing at the birth of Christ portrays things going on in the invisible realm, which at special seasons (like Christmas) are seen by man. The last days will be the most remarkable season of all time; thus, we can expect many angelic visitations.

Yes, angels helped many important people through the centuries. Yet, here is something you may not know. Angels also want to help you personally! Here's proof... "

What are...angels? They are spirits sent to serve those who are going to receive salvation" (Heb. 1:14).

If you're "going to receive salvation," you have at least one angel serving you! He may guard you against harm (You've heard of "guardian angels." See Acts 12:5, 18:10). He might warn you of impending danger. You'll likely need the comfort of his invisible presence. He might even visit you in a dream or a vision, as we read they did in the Bible.

Thus, as we close this important chapter about angels, ask yourself about your future, "Am I 'going to receive salvation?'" If unsure, you must read this book till the last page! An angel may be watching over you even now as you read!

3

Demons and Satan

"Fallen! Babylon the Great has fallen! She has become a home for demons. She is a prison for every evil spirit" (Rev. 18:2).

Demons are always looking for a home! (Are you inviting one into YOUR home?)

The world will fall into great confusion and deception in the last days. The Tower of Babel (confusion) was in ancient Babylon. This verse likens the conditions of the world at a future time to an ancient "fallen" city of confusion—a bewildered planet wide open to attacks from "every evil spirit."

Demons and Satan (the devil) will be very active during the fulfillment of Revelation, just as will good angels.

There are things you may not know about Satan. But the Word of God tells us much about him. He was at one time a Cherub angel named Lucifer, who was positioned above the throne of God. He was the grandest of all God's creations: "full of wisdom and perfect in beauty." However, he became filled with pride: **"You became too proud because of your beauty"** (Ezek. 28:12, 17).

For this sin, Lucifer was cast out of heaven. What a fantastic being he originally was! His beauty, wisdom, and influence convinced one-third of the heavenly angels to leave heaven with him: "(Satan's) **tail swept away one-third of the stars in the sky and threw them down to earth**" (Rev. 12:4). Notice again, angels were referred to as "stars." Many believe these fallen «stars» (angels who chose evil over good) became what we now call demons.

Earth then became Lucifer's haunt. As a "fallen angel," his name was changed to Satan, which means "adversary." He was also given many other titles in the Bible. Each one throws light on his evil character: The Accuser, Adversary, The Deceiver, The Dragon, The Enemy, Evil One, Liar, Murderer, Prince of the Power of the Air, Ruler of the Darkness, Ruler of this World, Serpent, Tempter, Thief, the Wicked One.

Satan is not very nice. As the first created being in the universe to sin, he originated sin. In the Garden of Eden, this "Deceiver" entered the body of an animal called a serpent (which, at that time, like a parrot, could speak). This snake tempted Eve to partake of the forbidden fruit, which God had warned would result in her death. The disguised devil lied to Eve and said, "You won't die." Sadly, she believed the devil's lie, ate, and eventually died, as all humanity since does. Eve's and, subsequently, Adam's sin became the greatest tragedy of human history and death became the great curse on our entire planet and all living things.

So, Satan and "his angels" (Matthew 25:41) have been behind evil worldly events for millennia. If you are battling any kind of evil today, this is how Ephesians 6:12 expresses it: **"For we are not fighting against flesh-and-blood enemies, but against evil rulers and authorities of the unseen world, against mighty powers in this dark world, and against evil spirits".**

Notice it does not mention Satan. There is only one Satan, and he can only be in one place at a time. Therefore, the devil has organized a functioning army of his evil subordinates. You may never personally have to contend with Satan himself. But watching the world today, he certainly has a well-trained army.

Reread the above verse closely. You've likely thought your present problem is a parent, a mate, a boss, a neighbor, or some politician. The Bible explains the REAL fight you are in is with invisible evil spirits, who both use or possess humans.

Satan's angels hate you. Why? Because you have a Savior, Jesus...that is, if you want Him. They are jealous of your future. The only future they have is Hell, described in Matt. 25:41 as: **"everlasting fire that was prepared for the devil and his angels"**

Most of your exposure to Satan and demons is likely from Hollywood film productions. Screenwriters often portray Satan as hideous, bright red, horned, with sharp teeth, cloven hoofs, and a pitchfork. I write about demons as one who has cast them out from many people.

Satan and demons are referred to as the **"Power of Darkness"** in Colossians 1:13. Hence, as we explore their power, we will uncover great darkness. Don't treat this study lightly! Let's first look at the inaccurate depictions of evil spirits Hollywood gives us; then, I'll share some of my experiences. Then the Bible will throw light on this dark subject. It exposes lies from the truth. **"If they speak not according to this word, it is because there is no light in them"** (Is. 8:20 KJV).

Hollywood movies seem to indicate demons:

- Are horrific monster-like beings

- Are ghosts of people who died

- Make people crawl on ceilings

- Like throwing priests out of windows

- Can be very big and strong

- Are to be greatly feared!

In my personal experience, most demons:

- Are more just rascally beings

- Are not very brave

- Are NEVER a dead person's ghost

- Can't make people do impossible things (like walking on ceilings or twisting their neck by 360 degrees)

- Are much weaker than ANY believing Christian

I never saw an evil spirit (Rarely do humans to see one), but I have dealt with demon possession for over four decades. Things I have observed people with demons do while I attempted an exorcism include:

- Spit, scream, gag, or vomit

- Wrestle with you, usually grabbing your clothes

- Run away from you

- Reach toward your neck to try to choke you (I was picked up and thrown against a wall, but only one time in these many years)

- Talk to you (using the person's voice, slightly strained)

- Try to scare you by making a fiendish face or saying such things as "I hate you! I'm going to kill you!"

Space doesn't allow more details, but I have written another book, *Miracles Are Your Destiny*. A section on demons and exorcism includes detailed stories from my years of casting out demons. It also includes testimonies from people dramatically transformed after their deliverance. If this chapter has made you curious, you can order my book from Amazon.com or Barnes & Noble.

We learned in the previous chapter there are at least 100 million angels. Since one-third of the angels fell with Satan, that means there are at least 50 or so million evil spirits, so our enemy has quite an army!

As we close this chapter, the most important thing to understand about demons is simply this–they lie! Satan invented lying: **"The devil...has always hated the truth, because there is no truth in him. When he lies, it is consistent with his character; for he is a liar and the father of lies"** (John 8:44 NLT).

Satan told Eve, "You won't die!"

What is the devil telling you? He uses what appear to be your own thoughts. Whatever he may be saying to you, know he is lying! Believing the devil's lie cost Eve her life. Do you believe in a lie that could cost you your life or even your soul? John 10:10 warns:

"The thief's purpose is to steal and kill and destroy."

Satan has a horrible plan for your life.

Don't let him kill you (with booze, drugs, or suicide). Don't let him steal your happiness, nor let him destroy your God-ordained destiny!

After first giving the John 10:10 warning, Jesus offers a beautiful alternative to the devil's plan:

"My purpose is to give them a rich and satisfying life."

Does that describe your life? If not, the Bible teaches it is Jesus' planned purpose for you.

Good things are ahead. But bad things are also! Revelation shows us there will be much "destruction" on Earth in the final days: destruction...like nuclear war!

Next, read about a fiery war that might soon come to a city near you!

4

Nuclear War

"One-third of the earth was burned up, one-third of the trees were burned up, and all the green grass was burned up" (Rev. 8:7).

On August 6, 1945, the Enola Gay B-29 bomber dropped the "Little Boy" atomic weapon on Hiroshima, Japan, resulting in an estimated 140,000 deaths. Those near "ground zero" were pulverized within a second. The nuclear explosion was the equivalent of 30,000,000 pounds of TNT! Fires broke out throughout the city. Many were burned and battered by the 7000-degree fireball. People cried out for water until what looked like "black rain" fell. Many filled their mouths with the quenching liquid, unaware the drops were highly radioactive and would bring them a painful death.

Because the Japanese refused to surrender, another atomic bomb dubbed "Fat Man" was soon dropped on Nagasaki. This resulted in the death of tens of thousands more. Japan, at last, surrendered, confronted with the undeniable reality of this new weapon. Thus began the "atomic arms race." The USA, Russia, France, Britain, China, India, and Pakistan all have nuclear weapons and ICBMs to deliver them. Israel may have a few, and North Korea has some. Most frightening, Iran may soon have them as well. China, bullying nearby nations and threatening Taiwan with war, has maybe 300 nuclear weapons. Pakistan is an Islamic country with an estimated 160+ warheads. Russia alone has over 6,000 nuclear warheads. On October 30, 1961, Russia detonated a nuclear bomb over 3,000 times as powerful as the bomb dropped on Hiroshima. The mushroom-like cloud from the explosion was 25 miles wide at its base and over 50 miles wide at its top. At 40 miles high, it was more than seven times higher than Mt. Everest, the world's tallest mountain. Everything within 36 miles of the impact was vaporized, and damage extended to a 150 miles radius. A weapon of this magnitude could quickly destroy New York City, Los Angeles, and their suburbs.

Paul prophesied in 2 Tim. 3:1 that in the last days:

"Perilous times shall come."

Is not this nuclear age a "perilous time?" Thousands of the most destructive nuclear weapons, many aimed at cities in America, are ready to be unleashed at the push of a button! Could some overthrow of a government or military coup by Muslim extremists place those weapons in the hands of terrorists?

In His discourse on the last days, Jesus said:

"Unless those days were shortened, there would be no flesh saved" (Matt. 24:22).

A worldwide nuclear war would unleash vast nuclear energy on Earth, causing immediate death, lingering death by radiation, and possible radical atmospheric disturbances. Such a war could result in an uninhabitable planet! It's a horrible prospect. Yet, it would give a very plausible explanation of Jesus' prophesy that "no flesh would be saved." But, Jesus said in v. 22: **"BUT for the elect's sake, those days shall be shortened."**

An angel will sound the last trumpet, and "the elect" (faithful followers of Christ) shall be delivered from this planet before such final destruction. (More about this in later chapters). Of course, this doesn't mean some cities or nations might yet experience a nuclear holocaust. It does mean the Lord will intervene and have the final word in the matter. And that word, thankfully, will be "No more destruction."

Also, wouldn't the millions killed and the destruction of whole cities by nuclear war perfectly fulfill Jesus' words in the previous chapter that Satan "comes to...kill and destroy?"

Jesus warned concerning the last days: **"Men's hearts shall fail them for fear, and for looking after those things which are coming on the earth: for the powers of heaven shall be shaken"** (Luke 21:26)

A nuclear explosion could fulfill the "powers of heaven" being "shaken." Hydrogen bombs use the same molecular reaction that fuels the energy-releasing power of the sun and the stars: nuclear fusion. Also, at the end of our planet, 2 Peter 2:10 (NKJV) describes: **"...the elements will melt with fervent heat; both the earth and the works that are in it will be burned up."**

I believe it is very likely the world will one day experience nuclear war because:

First, In bringing His judgment on wicked cities:

"The Lord made burning...fire rain out of heaven on Sodom and Gomorrah" (Gen. 19:24). Isn't that precisely what ICBMs do? Missiles from out of the heavens bring "burning!" God rained fire on two ancient cities, Sodom and Gomorrah. He could do it again to cities spreading wickedness like Hollywood, Las Vegas, or San Francisco.

I find encouragement from Gen. 18:16-33. God promised He would spare Sodom and Gomorrah if He could find just ten righteous souls living there. And there are far more than ten righteous souls in America.

Second, furthermore, there is no hint of the existence of the United States at the end of time in Revelation, Daniel, Isaiah, or other prophetic books. The scriptures refer to Europe, Asia, the Middle East, Israel, and Russia.

Today America is the world's most significant power financially and militarily. However, there appears to be no references to our nation. The United States has been a champion for freedom, protecting nations like Israel, fighting terrorism, and defeating antichrist-style leaders like Hitler. If America will play an essential part in the end-times, why are we not mentioned in end-time prophecies?

Frightening indeed is the specter America may not be mentioned in the scriptures because it will no longer be an influential nation. And I still can't get away from the nagging feeling America is not found in prophecy because we may be all but destroyed by nuclear war.

Third, Revelation 8:7 describes a scene that could easily be interpreted as nuclear explosions:

"The first angel sounded: And hail and fire followed, mingled with blood, and they were thrown to the earth; and a third of the trees were burned up, and all green grass was burned up."

A "third of the trees" being burned up certainly sounds like the effects of a nuclear holocaust! And one-third represents a lot of the earth's surface! Is America to be one of the two-thirds left, or are we a part of the one-third that experiences such devastation? I don't think we can say for sure, but I don't like the odds (only one out of three!).

When I was growing up in the '50s, in our grammar school in Southern California, we would have "Air Raid Drills." The bell would sound, and we students would climb under our little desks, pull our legs up under our bodies, and cover our heads and faces with our arms and hands. Why? So, when we were "pulverized" at 10,000 degrees Fahrenheit, at least we would be in a comfortable position?

No, there is little you can do to protect yourself against a thermonuclear explosion, and you can't outrun fallout. Yet, there is a lesson from history that can give you hope.

Before God rained fire upon Sodom and Gomorrah, angels came to the house of a righteous man, Lot. They warned him to leave the city and took him by the hand, and led him and his family out of the town before it was destroyed:

"When the morning dawned, the angels urged Lot to hurry, saying, "Arise, take your wife and your two daughters who are here, lest you be consumed in the punishment of the city. And while he lingered, the men took hold of his hand, his wife's hand, and the hands of his two daughters, the Lord being merciful to him, and they brought him out and set him outside the city" (Gen. 19:15-16).

Live for Christ, and God's angels could take you "by the hand" and help you to escape a fiery death!

In Daniel 3:20-30, three of God's followers were thrown into a fiery furnace by the wicked king of Babylon, Nebuchadnezzar. Their clothes did not burn. There wasn't even the odor of fire on them. And the king reportedly saw a fourth man in the fire who looked like "the Son of God" (V. 25, KJV). Put your faith in the Son of God. He could do the same for you during any future fire.

Rev. 16:8 (NKJV) prophesies: **"Then the fourth angel poured out his bowl on the sun, and power was given to him to scorch men with fire."**

Will the angel use the sun's power, hydrogen explosions, to "scorch men with fire?" Think about it

Thank God, this terrifying chapter could all be moot for you and me. Jesus may take His followers to heaven in the rapture (more about this in a later chapter) before one nuclear weapon ever falls!

Follow Christ, and you can escape ALL coming fires falling on earth (As well as an eternal fire, Hell!).

5

Graves

"I was dead, but now I am alive forever. I have the keys of death and Hell" (Jesus, Rev. 1:18).

Jesus died but rose again and walked out of His tomb three days later. He now has "the keys of death and Hell." Those keys will open every grave, including yours. You aren't dead yet, but you can learn a lot in this chapter to help prepare yourself for that hour.

Revelation reveals death plays a BIG role in the coming end times. Death and other forms of the word (dead, die, died, and the related words kill and killed) are mentioned fifty-four times in the book. Before we look more closely at what St. John said, let's see what other people "think" about death and their grave.

Edvard Munch, the Norwegian painter, said,

"From my rotting body, flowers shall grow, and I am in them, and that is eternity."

Poetic, but I doubt Edvard found any personal comfort from his theology after his death!

It's reported Actor/Singer Frank Sinatra was buried with Tootsie Rolls, a pack of Camels, a Zippo lighter, and a bottle of Jack Daniels. I'm sure Frank enjoyed his gifts six feet. under, in the dark, surrounded by his expensive, pretty casket!

Death? Most people don't get it! Otherwise, why would we put a pillow in a casket for the departed to rest his head?

Hugh Hefner, Playboy Magazine founder, was buried in the crypt he had purchased, located directly beside Actress Marilyn Monroe's crypt. I'm sure Hugh enjoys watching her "beautiful" rotting corpse!

One man had a glass window put on his casket with an open tube clear to the surface. He also had them put a string in his coffin attached to a bell above the ground so if he was buried alive and "woke" up, he could let people know to come to rescue him. I promise you that bell never rang.

Are you expecting to be buried or cremated when you die? It won't make a bit of difference. After Adam's fall, the Lord informed him:

"By the sweat of your brow, you will produce food to eat until you return to the ground, because you were taken from it. You are dust, and you will return to dust" (Genesis 3:19).

Think you prefer burial? My dad worked at a cemetery. Once, he had to dig up someone dead for decades to bury him elsewhere. When they opened the casket, guess what was inside? *Just one big bone!* The rest had disintegrated, as prophesied to Adam.

What about cremation? My dad had another story to tell. It seems an older man had been planning to have his body cremated. So, dressed up in a suit, he came to where my dad worked and asked if he could see how the cremation process worked. My dad said, "Sure," and took him to the basement, where they happened to have someone being cremated at that very moment!

There was a little window in the door so workers could see how the burning of the body was progressing. The curious man glanced through the window and began screaming and running back up the stairs, terrified. (I think we can assume he decided to NOT be cremated).

If you do choose cremation, just remember this...

After you meet your cremator,
   you'll soon meet your Creator!

It is crucial to understand all you can about death since

"Everyone must die once" (Heb. 9:27 GNT).

Wise Solomon said we don't take anything with us when we die, not even our clothes:

"They came from their mother's womb naked. They will leave as naked as they came. They won't even be able to take a handful of their earnings with them from all their hard work" (Eccl. 5:15).

A rich man died. Upon hearing of his death, someone asked a co-worker, "How much did he leave?" His response: "All of it!" I've performed around 300 funerals, and not once have I seen a U-Haul trailer following a hearse. Every rich man who ever lived, at death, left everything behind. Should you worry about getting it now if you can't take it with you?

A bumper sticker read,

"He who dies with the most toys wins!"

Ridiculous! Jesus clarified:

"Life is not about having a lot of material possessions" (Luke 12:15).

Death is a final departure from life on earth. I have watched three people die (A friend in the hospital, a relative on their deathbed, and one drunken stranger, hit by a van and dying in the street). Death is VERY convincing.

I heard a comedian suggest if you want to go to a funeral and show your dislike for a person, sit in the service eating popcorn and Coke. We all would like to think there'd be a few tears shed at our funeral, but not tears from laughter.

Have you ever considered what you would like relatives to inscribe on your headstone? Here are rather humorous epitaphs taken from tombstones and grave markers:

"The children of Israel wanted bread, and the Lord sent them manna. Old clerk Wallace wanted a wife, and the Devil sent him Anna." (*From Ribbesford, England*)

"I don't want to talk about it right now." (*Bonnie Anderson*)

"That's All Folks." (*Mel Blanc-the voice for Bugs Bunny*)

"Stranger tread this ground with gravity. Dentist Brown is filling his last cavity." (*On a dentist's grave marker*)

"Going. Going. Gone!" (*Jedediah Goodwin-Auctioneer*)

"Pardon me for not rising." (*John Yeast*)

"Here lies the body of Jonathan Blake. Stepped on the gas instead of the brake." (From Uniontown, PA)

"All dressed up and no place to go." (*On an atheist's tombstone*)

Following are from unknown locations or persons ...

"Here lies Pa. Pa liked wimin. Ma caught Pa in with two swimmin. Here lies Pa."

"Here lies old Aunt Hannah Proctor, who purged but didn't call the Doctor: She couldn't stay; she had to go. Praise God from whom all blessings flow."

Also, think about this: what will be your last words? Here are some humorous reported last words...

(Groucho Marx, comedian): **"Die, my dear? Why, that's the last thing I'll do!"**

(*When asked if he had any last requests before facing a firing squad, James W. Rodgers said*): **"Yes...A bullet-proof vest!"**

Most people, for obvious reasons, don't feel like being funny at their death. Frank Sinatra's last words were: **"I'm losing!"**

Reminds me of Jesus' words in Mark 8:36:

"For what will it profit a man if he gains the whole world, and loses his own soul?"

Death is life's way of telling you, "You're fired!" When you are fired, how are you going to die?

For some, death is an awful experience. Consider the following (unsubstantiated but apparently factual) ways some have died:

- A poodle fell from a balcony in Argentina in 1988, killing three people. One was struck on the head, one was run over by a bus while watching, and the third witnessed the event and had a heart attack

- 2500+ left-handed people are killed annually by using products designed for right-handed people

- Since 1978, at least 37 people have tragically died because of shaking vending machines too violently in an attempt to get free merchandise

- More people are killed annually by donkeys than die in air crashes

- More die by falling coconuts than sharks

- In the 90s, 37 jet airplane mechanics servicing engines were accidentally sucked into the engines and expelled in tiny chunks

- 500 die in the U.S. annually from bee stings

Indeed, there are many ways to end up in a grave, aren't there? You can't do a lot about determining how your physical body dies. Still, you can manage how you die emotionally and spiritually.

"Falling into the hands of the living God is a terrifying thing" (Heb. 10:31).

To die without knowing Christ as your personal Savior is a frightful thing! Death is our enemy. Death is ugly. The Bible calls the grave "cruel." But followers of Christ can have complete confidence in avoiding Hell, assured death is but an instant passageway into a far better place:

"We are confident, yes, well pleased rather to be absent from the body and to be present with the Lord" (2 Cor. 5:8 NKJV).

When a sincere Christian dies, his soul immediately leaves his body and goes to be "present with the Lord." Paul wrote in Phil. 1:21-23 (NKJV):

"For to me, to live is Christ, and to die is gain."

Paul said he desired (more than life itself) to:

"...depart and be with Christ, which is far better"

If you are not right with God and fear falling into His hands in judgment, get right with Him today!

In the movie "Ghost," as evil people die, we see demons from Hell rising from the inferno to drag their souls down to the pit. But since demons helped further an evil soul's journey toward hell, God isn't going to give them that pleasure! It is actually the angels that do this:

"...at the end of time. The Son of Man will send his angels. They will gather...everyone who does evil. The angels will throw them into a blazing furnace" (Matt. 13:40-42).

Angels carried a dying righteous man named Lazarus to Paradise (Luke 16:22). If you follow Christ at death, you'll have the privilege of seeing heavenly angels coming your way to guide and welcome you into heaven. This thought has encouraged people for many centuries! Even mistreated enslaved Americans used to sing,

> *"I looked over Jordan, And WHAT did I see,*
> *Comin' for to carry me home,*
> *A band of angels comin' after me.*
> *Comin' for to carry me home."*

Where is your eternal home? If it is heaven, you also can joyfully sing that chorus!

On a man's tombstone were inscribed these words,

"Now I know something you don't."

Immediately after death, you will either know all about Heaven or all about Hell. Finish this book to perhaps learn "something you don't know," so there won't be any unpleasant eternal surprises ahead of you.

6

DEATH

"I looked, and there was a pale horse, and its rider's name was Death. Hell followed him. They were given power over one-fourth of the earth to kill people using wars, famines, plagues, and the wild animals on the earth" (Rev. 6:8).

Chapter 6 pictures what has been called "The four horsemen of the Apocalypse." When John describes the four riders, he doesn't give three of them specific names. But he does call the rider on the pale horse "DEATH" as though he is a living being with a name (and a horrible name at that).

One-fourth of the population of the earth will be killed by DEATH.

With approximately eight billion people on earth today, one-fourth of these would be two billion! Suppose these deaths take place evenly across the continents. In that case, it would mean, in America, the equivalent of the entire population of California, Oregon, Washington, Nevada, Utah, Colorado, Arizona, and New Mexico would be killed.

Rev. 6:8 says death will come by four methods:

Wars: DEATH kills by causing wars. Over 50 million died in World War II! We can easily envision war (especially with nuclear weapons) resulting in many, many millions of deaths!

Famine: But DEATH also kills by "famine." (Other translations say "hunger"). Jesus said in Luke 21:11 there would be "famine" in the last days. That shouldn't be hard to believe. Currently, "795 million people do not have enough food to lead a healthy, active life. Poor nutrition causes nearly half (45%) of deaths in children under five" (Source: world food program, wfp.org).

In 1769-1773 a famine in Bengal (Now named India and Bangladesh) killed 10 million people, one-third of the population! If one-third of the world's current population were destroyed by famine, it would be about 2.67 billion dead! One-third of America would mean over 110,000,000 dead.

Revelation 8:7 predicts one-third of the trees and grass will be burned up. I hardly think one-third of trees and grass would be burned up, yet corn, wheat, and beans would be spared! And, if one-third of the world's grain, vegetable, and fruit crops were destroyed, wouldn't that equal one-third of the population with nothing to eat? Famine is coming, maybe not today or tomorrow, but God's Word may soon be fulfilled.

Most Americans have never really known hunger. But things can change. And they will rapidly once the horseman called DEATH is unleashed on earth through.

Plagues: (also called pestilences) are contagious, and widespread, infectious diseases which result in many deaths. There have been many plagues throughout history.

- The Black Death (Bubonic Plague) in the 14th century killed half the population of Europe

- The 1918 Spanish Flu killed 675,000 Americans (including my paternal grandfather)

- HIV/AIDS (1981-today) killed at least 27 million

- Covid19 (2019-today) has killed over nearly seven million, with over one million deaths in the U.S.A. alone. And there's no end in sight

Animals: Mankind has always been subject to Death from animals. Animals estimated to cause some of the most deaths worldwide among humans each year are...

Mosquitoes 1,000,000

Snakes 50,000

Dogs 25,000

Crocodiles 1,000

Hippopotamus 500

Elephants 100

Lions 100

Cows 22

Wolves............................10

Sharks 10

In addition, many bacterial diseases begin in and are spread by animals. Some believe Covid19 was spread by bats. The HIV/AIDS epidemic began in Chimpanzees. The Black Plague is thought to have been spread by rats. Now we have Monkeypox. What's up next? Rev. 6:8 mentions death by:

"...the wild animals on the earth."

We read in the news pets can turn unexpectedly on their owners and kill them. Imagine an end-time scenario where the entire animal kingdom rises against humans. Pet snakes slithering through bedrooms to kill their owners. Pet birds spreading a new "bird flu" that, in past years, killed hundreds but ultimately kills millions. Because of famine, starving domestic animals, like cats and dogs, suddenly realize the only way they will stay alive is with the help of their "master's" flesh.

Matt. 8:30-32) tells the story of two demon-possessed men living in the tombs. When Jesus commanded the demons to come out, they begged Jesus to allow them to enter the bodies of a nearby herd of pigs. Jesus permitted them, and the demons drove the pigs wild until they all ran into the sea and drowned. Demons from Hell could be unleashed to enter domesticated animals, driving them to do things they'd never usually do, like kill people.

DEATH will be the ruthless agent of deaths by the animal kingdom, wars, famines, and plagues. The damage caused will be so terrifying that 8:15 says:

"Then the kings of the earth, the important people, the generals, the rich, the powerful, and all the slaves and free people hid themselves in caves and among the rocks in the mountains."

Yet, whatever disasters are ahead, if you love God, you can hope to be safe, yet fearlessly face DEATH, if necessary, if you will but believe these promises:

"Because you love me, I will rescue you. I will protect you because you know my name. When you call to me, I will answer you. I will be with you when you are in trouble. I will save you and honor you. I will satisfy you with a long life" (Psalm 91:14-16).

7

The Beast

"I saw the souls of those whose heads had been cut off because of their testimony about Jesus and because of the word of God. They had not worshiped the beast or its statue and were not branded on their foreheads or hands" (Rev. 20:4).

In the last days, many will be beheaded because they refuse to worship "the beast." The picture of the guillotine is a sobering reminder of this time—massive death for those who will not follow a last-day leader's religion. A beast indeed! Who is this beast?

"I saw a beast coming out of the sea...And the serpent (Satan) **gave its power, kingdom, and far-reaching authority to the beast."** (Rev. 13:1, 2).

There are over 380 movies about monsters. Horror films are almost a sure box-office success. But, no movie monster could ever compare to a "monster" mentioned in Revelation. In his first two biblical letters (1 John, 2 John), John refers to this monstrous beast as the "Antichrist."

"...the Antichrist is coming" (1 John 2:18 NKJV).

Arnold Schwarzenegger's movie, End of Days, is the story of a cop who tries to keep a woman from being impregnated by the devil to give birth to the Antichrist. Walt Disney's FX TV series "Little Demon" featured a woman impregnated by Satan who gave birth to an Antichrist daughter. There are many more like these.

Hollywood often fictionalizes biblical themes to draw a wider audience. Their take on the Antichrist is usually fantasy and not at all biblical. But God's Word is NEVER fantasy. Antichrist means "against Christ" or, as some translations say, "the enemy of Christ." In the book of Revelation, John no longer referred to him by that title but rather as a "beast," in 13:2:

"The beast that I saw was like a leopard. Its feet were like a bear's feet. Its mouth was like a lion's mouth."

This is a metaphorical description of a beast-like man. Daniel 8:23 says of the Antichrist:

"When the end of those kingdoms is near and they have become so wicked that they must be punished, there will be a stubborn, vicious, and deceitful king."

"The end" is when "they (the nations) have become so wicked they must be punished." Evil will be so rampant on the earth it will provide a vacuum for someone who is "stubborn, vicious, and deceitful" to rise to power. He will be a "king" (So, he is a visible world leader, a man). And he will perfectly personify sin:

"...that Day (The second coming of Christ) **will not come unless the falling away comes first, and the MAN OF SIN is revealed, the son of perdition"** (2 Thess. 3:3).

The "falling away" refers to the last day rebellion or a time of great apostasy (a departure from the truth). Notice, again, the Antichrist is "a man," however, a particular kind of man: "a man of sin." Jesus died to deliver us from our sins, so the man "against Christ" wants to deceive mankind into ever deeper sin.

Notice he is also called "the son of perdition." ("the one doomed to destruction" NIV) There are only two people in the Bible called this. One is Judas (in John 17:12), and the other is the Antichrist. Judas went to Hell for his betrayal of Christ. The beast is also going to Hell for his betrayal of Christ. Satan entered Judas, as we learned earlier. And Satan will also enter the beast...

"The man of sin will come with the power of Satan. He will use every kind of power, including miraculous and wonderful signs. But they will be lies" (2 Thess. 2:9).

The Antichrist will exercise great powers and will not work alone. His personal aide is "the false prophet" (Rev. 19:20):

"He (the false prophet) **performs great signs, so that he even makes fire come down from heaven on the earth in the sight of men"** (Rev. 13:13 NKJV).

One of his "great signs" will be to cause a statue built in the Antichrist's honor to appear to become alive:

"He was granted power to give breath to the image of the beast, that the image of the beast should ...speak" (Rev. 13:15 NKJV).

In the past, this would have sounded fantastic, but not anymore. Artificial Intelligence (AI) has advanced to the degree computers can talk. Some researchers in artificial intelligence predict soon-coming "human-level machine intelligence," or HLMI.

Computers handle our money, answer phones, call us, and speak to us. (For years, I would say "No thank you" when a computerized call center would ask me if I had any further business...that is until I realized I was saying "thank you" to a lifeless computer!)

The" image of the beast" will do more than speak:

"He was granted the power to give breath to the image" (13:15).

I suspect "breath" will be another deceiving miracle. A demon could possess the statue and imitate "the breathing." The purpose of this speaking, "breathing" computer is sinister:

"It also forced all people... to receive a mark on their right hands or on their foreheads. No one could buy or sell without this mark, which is the name of the beast or the number of its name" (13:16, 17).

What is that number? Verse 18 says it is (Can you guess it?)...

"666"

Notice it "forced all people." The time will come when the beast will compel everyone to decide whether or not to take "the mark of the beast." Modern computers can control your personal records (from bank, to DMV, to voting, etc.). They could also be utilized to demand and keep tabs on those who have complied with the unholy trinity's (the Antichrist, the false prophet, and the image of the beast) command to receive a 666 or the beast's name on the right-hand or forehead.

The technology is already here for this to happen. I often fly in my ministry and have a "Clear" membership. At the airport, I walk up to a machine and look into a camera (that reads my iris!) or put two fingers on a fingerprint reader. When the computer is convinced, I'm Dea Warford, attendants escort me to the front of the line.

"No one could buy or sell without this mark" (17).

During the Covid 19 outbreak, we learned to stand in line at grocery stores, come at certain hours, or buy a limited amount of certain products. Some stores had to close, while others remained open. Our government was controlling who bought and sold. So, the above prediction should not be hard to believe.

This evil plan requires a mark on the forehead or the hand (Similar to what even cell phones use to identify us). This mark then becomes an evident sign we are worshippers of the image of the beast. And if we refuse the mark or refuse to worship the image?

"He (the false prophet)...**causes as many as would not worship the image of the beast to be killed"** (13:15).

The day may soon come when everyone, including you and me, must decide. Will we take the mark to buy food or keep our businesses open? Or will we risk our families starving to death? Even more critical, will we worship a false idol, a demon, or will we worship the only true God? Heaven or Hell is in the balance!

"If anyone worships the beast and his image, and receives his mark on his forehead or on his hand, he himself shall also drink of the wine of the wrath of God, which is poured out full strength into the cup of His indignation. He shall be tormented with fire and brimstone in the presence of the holy angels and in the presence of the Lamb. And the smoke of their torment ascends forever and ever; and they have no rest day or night, who worship the beast and his image, and whoever receives the mark of his name" (Rev. 14:9-11).

Suppose you receive a "robocall" asking you to get an appointment at your local hospital or city hall to receive the Antichrist's mark on your forehead or hand. Will you be able to say "No?" Or if there's a knock at your door and the beast's "Gestapo" demands you take his mark then and there, will you be able to say "No?" That "no" could send you to the guillotine! (But it could also take you to heaven!)

The Lord gave us Revelation to help the last generation prepare for this dreadful time of the Beast.

Are you ready for that knock on your door?

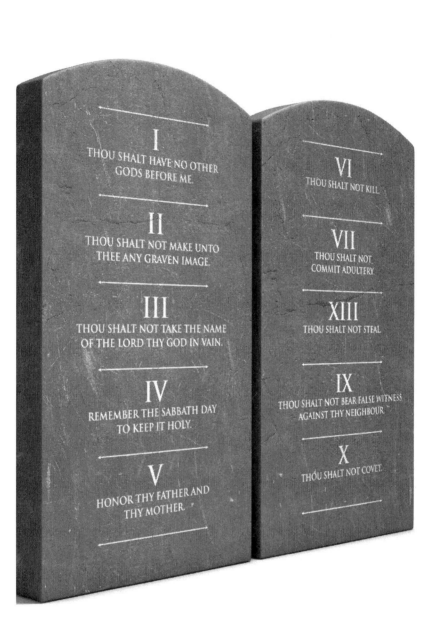

8

Four Deadly Sins

"The people who survived these plagues still did not turn to me and change...They did not turn away from committing murder, practicing witchcraft, sinning sexually, or stealing" (Rev. 9:20,21).

Sin is Earth's big problem. Sin is why Christ died for people and why you and I need a Savior. When we think of sin, we usually think of the Ten Commandments but those are not the only sins. Some sins are far worse than others.

"All wrongdoing is sin, but there is sin that is not deadly" (1 John 5:17 NRSVUE).

Everyone is guilty of "wrongdoing." And at times we all say and do things we know we shouldn't. But during the closing years of this age, four sins (deadly to the soul!) are mentioned as especially prevalent sins which, despite horrific things happening on earth, men will not "turn away from." Those sins are murder, witchcraft, sexual sin, and stealing. Let's take a closer look and see how the current events in our nation reveal how common these sins, which are so evil in God's eyes, have become.

1. Committing Murder...

I am quite sure you don't think murder is a good thing, but the daily news is filled with reports of some who thought it was, at least, a good idea for them. I doubt you are contemplating murder, but let me ask you this. Are you now, or have you ever contemplated suicide? Suicide IS the sin of murder. And Revelation reveals suicide attempts will become commonplace in the last days:

"At that time people will look for death and never find it. They will long to die, but death will escape them" (Rev. 9:6).

Each year in America, nearly 50,000 people "long to die" by taking their own lives! In about the time it takes to read this chapter, one person will have committed suicide!

Life on earth during the last days will be the most difficult mankind has ever known. So, is suicide an option when life gets especially hard? It is NOT! There is no question, in God's eyes, suicide is a sin. And it is one of the most selfish things anyone could possibly do: to leave loved ones behind to find and dispose of a body and to grieve over that death for the rest of their lives, often wondering whether there was something they should have done that might have prevented this. I know a man personally who found the body of his son, who had hanged himself. Parents can only imagine what it might be like: the grotesque expression on his face; the blackened skin; the sleepless nights of agonizing, "How could I have not seen he was struggling so. What did I do wrong? What did I fail to do, as his parent, to prevent this?" Years later, I asked that father to what degree his pain had lessened. "If the pain level was a ten then, what is it now?" "Eleven!" The grieving father had to go on Prozac to get any sleep.

And, as for suicide, the Lord took me out of the ministry and put me in a job shoveling hot sand at the foundry of Kaiser Steel in Fontana, CA, when I was about 30. I was under such stress I was passing blood. I fought depression. While driving home after putting in a double shift (from 8 A.M. to nearly 12 A.M.), I looked at my speedometer and the concrete overpass pylons along the freeway and thought: "Hmm, 70 miles an hour. If I would just pull this car into that pylon, all these troubles would be forever behind me." I, at last, understood why people commit suicide.

Yet, what a satanic "device" suicide is. After having to cast demons out of many people plagued with thoughts of suicide, I know the devil often has much to do with suicide. Yet, neither Satan nor demons can make anybody commit suicide. They can harass them with such thoughts: "You don't deserve to live. Just jump! Take that bottle of drugs, and you'll just go to sleep. Then, your problems will be forever over." But, ultimately, man's choice can be overruled by neither demons nor God himself (because God created man with free will).

Hollywood, (As a metaphor for the media, music, TV, and the movie industry) is Satan's greatest tool to corrupt the minds of Americans. One of the finest examples of this is the way it portrays suicide. We see people committing suicide in movies because it seems the only way out or it's the "honorable thing to do," or it's one's way of saying, "This is all somebody like me deserves," or it's the ultimate method to scream, "I can't take it anymore."

Often, suicide marks the end of a life of depression, pain, or unhappiness, and Hollywood seems to intimate there are times this is okay. This is Hollywood fantasyland. But we are living in the REAL world. It is during the Great Tribulation many will try to take Hollywood's example of a way out of suffering, suicide. But God has a surprise for them. What does Rev. 9:6 mean when it says, "At that time people will look for death and never find it. They will long to die, but death will escape them." We don't know for sure, but what an amazing picture! Can you imagine a man putting a gun to his head, and it's jammed? Can you imagine someone taking a bottle of sleeping pills, saying "Goodbye cruel world" one last time, and then waking up at 11 A.M., still alive in the same cruel world, only with a splitting headache and vomiting?

Perhaps the angels, who are mentioned so often in Revelation, will personally be preventing suicide during the Tribulation. Hollywood may say, "It's the easy way out!" But God will, in essence, be saying, "Not so fast! This is my time of dealing with my creation's stubbornness and sin. People aren't getting out so quickly and easily!"

Is suicide the way out? Not on your life! That suicide is thought to be an easy way out is but a deception! To leave family and friends to mourn over your loss, to pre-empt God's destined purpose for your life, and to likely wake up in Hell! What irony! To think one could take his life to avoid the hardships of this world, only to wake up in an infinitely worse one! If you are ever tempted to commit suicide, remind yourself of this fact!

Satan, through Hollywood, Facebook, Tik Tok, and the like, has influenced a new generation of youth who now experiment with "playing chicken," cutting, strangling themselves for a sexual high, playing Russian Roulette, and taking deadly drugs. Satan may invent other last-day evil tools of destruction. Hollywood "glamorizes" such things, which often can result in accidental suicide. Once more, suicide, killing oneself, is nothing less than murder! And what happens in the end to murderers?

"murderers...will find themselves in the fiery lake of burning sulfur. This is the second death" (Rev. 21:8).

"The second death" is infinitely worse than any method on earth bringing a first death (of the physical body), including suicide! When Earth's events finally get terrible, the one thing you don't want to do is try to escape by suicide. It would be the ultimate fulfillment of the proverbial jumping out of the frying pan into the fire! Don't jump into the fire! Stay here, at least a little longer!

Three Other Deadly Sins

Murder (including suicide) is listed along with three other very serious sins which we must study from the viewpoint of God, the author of the Bible, regardless of how trivial (and normal) Hollywood might depict them:

2. Witchcraft

Things like black magic, enchantment necromancy, the occult, conjuring, or fortune-telling are big in the entertainment industry. Many Americans explore witchcraft through astrology, palm reading, hypnotism, crystal balls, potions, and casting spells or curses. The Word of God generically calls these forbidden activities "witchcraft," Your Creator strictly forbids them. Why? Because Satan is the inventor and the power behind witchcraft. How do you know if you are guilty in God's eyes of this sin? "Any attempt to enter the realm of the Supernatural, except through Jesus Christ, is witchcraft" (Evangelist Mario Murillo).

In the Old Testament, the penalty for being a witch was death. Why such strict punishment? Satan aims to deceive people, control them, and ultimately drag them to Hell. This is exactly what he will do through the reign of the antichrist. The Lord loves you and doesn't want you to end up in the same Hell as the devil. So, he gives ample warning to avoid witchcraft.

I have cast many demons out of those who were involved in witchcraft. I have heard demons laugh like a witch as they departed from unwitting bodies. Some scream. Others use a subject's face to make a monstrous grin like in a horror movie. I see where Hollywood gets its inspiration!

If you, in the past, have delved into such things, repent of them. Renounce witchcraft. Throw away any books or paraphernalia you might have in your house. Find a pastor or strong Christian who can help you cast out any demons that might have been haunting your house (with odd manifestations) or disturbing you with depression or fear (symptoms of an evil invisible presence in your life). Google for help, "Deliverance minister near me." Or, email me at evangelist@deawarford.org. I want to help you.

"They did not turn away from...witchcraft...they which do such things shall not inherit the kingdom of God" (Galatians 5:20-21 KJV).

Want to "inherit the kingdom of God" instead of Hell? Repent and renounce witchcraft!

3. Sexual Impurity

Many of those around you who are your age may be having some kind of sexual relationship without being legally married. Society may accept it. But does God? The Bible says **"I, the Lord, never change"** (Mal. 3:6). **"Jesus Christ is the same yesterday, today, and forever"** (Heb. 13:8). **"O Lord, your word is established in heaven forever"** (Ps. 119:89). The God of today is the same God of many centuries ago when He destroyed Sodom and Gomorrah. Fire rained from heaven on cities whose inhabitants continue, even now, burning in eternal fire.

"Remember Sodom and Gomorrah, and the nearby towns, whose people...indulged in sexual immorality and perversion: they suffer the punishment of eternal fire as a plain warning to all" (Jude 1:7).

The only acceptable sexual relations, in God's eyes, were always, and are still today, those between a married man and woman.

"Marriage is honorable in every way, so husbands and wives should be faithful to each other. God will judge those who commit sexual sins" (Heb. 13:4).

"...in order to avoid sexual sins, each man should have his own wife, and each woman should have her own husband" (1 Cor. 7:2).

America's attitude may have changed, but God cannot and will not change. The late Evangelist Billy Graham said, "If God doesn't judge America, he'll have to apologize to Sodom and Gomorrah." God judges individuals, nations, or a planet when sin is so rampant and of such a harmful nature that it will continue to consume until it must be put to an end. The "burning fires of lust," I fear, will result in a coming destruction among those deceived thereby.

It is not too late. You still have time, at least today!

"I gave her time to turn to me and change the way she thinks and acts, but she refuses to turn away from her sexual sins" (Rev. 2:21).

Change the way you think (Don't deceive yourself that "it must not be that bad anymore because so many are doing it this way"). And change the way you act (Cease any sexual sins outside of marriage). Why? Because...

"But as for the...sexually immoral...their portion will be in the lake that burns with fire and sulfur, which is the second death" (Rev. 21:8). Repent today and get out of any sexually immoral relationships.

4. Theft

In May 2020, George Floyd was killed while being detained by cops in Minneapolis. Rioting, burning, and pillaging began there and spread to cities throughout America. Thieves began walking into stores while they were still open and filling bags with items, and walking out without paying for them. Most businesses didn't want their employees to try to restrain them, lest someone get hurt. Then, state and local governments stopped police from arresting shoplifters. This only emboldened more thieves to do the same. Many stores, even large national stores like Walgreens and Walmart, have closed because of widespread stealing.

If the richest nation in the world, America, can't keep its citizens from stealing, it is easy to see how when Revelation prophesies a time of great scarcity and famine, one of the most pronounced sins of that time will be theft. Here again, is where God has not changed his mind about this sin.

"Thou shalt not steal" is one of the Ten Commandments. Do not be among those who...

"neither repented...of their thefts." Here is why:

"...thieves...who rob people will not inherit the kingdom of God" (1 Cor. 6:10).

Have you stolen anything? Repent before God—pledge to never do it again. Make restitution wherever it is possible.

You personally may not have a problem with the sins mentioned in this chapter, but you do have a problem with sin. The Bible says so...

"All have sinned" (Romans 3:23).

That "all" includes YOU! And because you have sinned,

"...the payment for sin is death" (Romans 6:23).

Don't stop reading, as I'll show you in the last chapter how to receive forgiveness of any and every sin you have ever committed. For today, be aware of and ready to avoid especially flagrant sins that will rule the coming fallen world for a short, end-time season: murder (and suicide), witchcraft, sexual sin, and stealing.

9

The Rapture

"Look! He comes with the clouds of heaven. And everyone will see him—even those who pierced him. And all the nations of the world will mourn for him" (Rev. 1:7 NLT).

For 2000 years, Christians have anticipated Christ's return to earth. Each generation hoped He would come during their lifetime. He didn't. However, this current generation is different. Virtually all the signs the Bible warned about are occurring NOW! Christ's coming is referred to as "The Rapture." That is when Jesus returns from heaven and His true followers rise to meet Him in the air to begin their eternal life.

The reign of the Antichrist will be, at most, a few years. Many feel it will either be 3 ½ or 7 years. Yet, at some point, when the Antichrist is alive on earth, the most dramatic event in history will occur! The Rapture!

You doubtless know Christ's return is highly anticipated by the 1.5 billion Christians throughout the world. Following are some interesting things about His return that are important to understand...

1. "Everyone will see Him" (As Rev. 1:7 explains)

This will not be a private showing. How will every person on earth see Him? Do you know anybody who doesn't have a cell phone or a TV? Talk about something going viral! Try the Creator of the Universe returning to Earth! But then, as God, He would have no difficulty finding another way for everyone to see His return. Jesus said,

"The Son of Man will come again just as lightning flashes from east to west" (Matt. 24:27).

The "flashes" of light seen when lightning strikes, travel at the speed of light, 270,000,000 MPH. That means the flash could go worldwide seven times in one second! So, this could be a hint that the entire earth's population will see Christ's arrival in a moment, like a lightning flash from east to west!

2. No one knows exactly when Jesus Christ will return...

...though many have predicted the day. Followers of would-be prophets have sold all their goods and moved to the desert or mountains in anticipation of the Lord's arrival. Of course, they were all wrong and made fools of themselves. If they had just read the Bible, they wouldn't have followed anyone who claimed to know the time Jesus returns. This is why God gave us the Scriptures,

"No one knows when that day or hour will come" (Mark 13:32).

We can't know the "day" or the "hour" but we can know the approximate time because...

3. There will be many "signs" indicating we should expect the Lord's soon return. Jesus said,

"Nation will go to war against nation, and kingdom against kingdom. There will be great earthquakes, and there will be famines and plagues in many lands, and there will be terrifying things and great miraculous signs from heaven... And here on earth the nations will be in turmoil, perplexed...People will be terrified at what they see coming upon the earth... Then everyone will see the Son of Man coming... So when all these things begin to happen, stand and look up" (Luke 21: 10-11, 25-28 NLT).

Paul the Apostle added in 2 Tim. 3:1:

"In the last days there will be violent periods of time."

(This is exactly how God described the earth before Noah's flood destroyed all life.)

Then Paul went on in verses 2-5 to add:

"People will be selfish and love money. They will brag, be arrogant, and use abusive language. They will curse their parents, show no gratitude, have no respect for what is holy, and lack normal affection for their families. They will refuse to make peace with anyone. They will be slanderous, lack self-control, be brutal, and have no love for what is good. They will be traitors. They will be reckless and conceited. They will love pleasure rather than God. They will appear to have a godly life, but they will not let its power change them."

These signs are virtually everywhere today. Have you "let His power change" you?

4. Warnings to prepare have been given us

Even though we don't know exactly when the Lord will come, we can still live in anticipation, readiness, and preparedness:

"I'm coming soon! I will bring my reward with me to pay all people based on what they have done" (Rev. 22:12).

"Be ready, because the Son of Man will return when you least expect him" (Luke 12:40).

5. Very special things take place on that day

"The Lord will come from heaven with a command, with the voice of the archangel, and with the trumpet (call) of God. First, the dead who believed in Christ will come back to life. Then, together with them, we who are still alive will be taken in the clouds to meet the Lord in the air" (1 Thess. 4:16-17).

An angel will give the alarm! A heavenly trumpet will sound, reverberating across the universe! The dead bodies of those who served Christ will rise from the grave first, and their spirits will descend from heaven with Christ and reenter their resurrection bodies.

Then, every other Christian who prepared himself for that destined moment will also rise in their transformed physical body to "meet the Lord in the air." It is the crowning event of all time! Jesus comments about this divine moment:

"So remember what you received and heard. Obey, and change the way you think and act. If you're not alert, I'll come like a thief. You don't know when I will come (Rev. 3:3).

Will you go up on that day when He comes? Make your reservation!

10

Heaven

"I heard a loud voice from the throne say, "God lives with humans! God will make his home with them, and they will be his people. God himself will be with them and be their God" (Rev. 21:3).

The devil has used Hollywood to paint a picture of heaven as something floating around in clouds in fog. Eastern religions hint of a kind of nebulous existence where there is peace and "oneness with the universe." In Buddhism, "Nirvana" is a transcendent state in which there is neither suffering, desire, nor sense of self, and the subject is released from the effects of karma and the cycle of death and rebirth. It is the final goal of Buddhism. Who wants to spend eternity in a place like that!

In 2 Cor. 12:2, Paul spoke of being taken to the "third heaven." The first heaven would likely be our atmosphere, the second heaven outer space, and the "third heaven" the place where God and His angels dwell. When we speak of dying and "going to heaven," we simply mean we are going where God is. Then we get to see the Father for the first time. We are "married to the Lord" at the "Marriage Supper of the Lamb." (See Rev. 19:9).

Yeah! We get to eat in heaven! Bet it's Mexican Food! Christians will sit at the "Judgment Seat of Christ," at which time we receive our crowns and heavenly rewards.

Then, after a time of celebration and receiving our rewards, we all come back with Christ to earth for what is called The Millennium. We will live on earth for a thousand years (See Rev. 20:4). All the things we didn't enjoy during our short life on earth will be available to all. Visit Africa. See Paris. This is when the seemingly inequities of life become fair. Children who died young, parents killed in accidents, severely handicapped, will get to make up for a few years of suffering with a thousand years of pleasures.

The Word says a lot about the rewards of His followers. First, just as in Hell there are degrees of punishment (See Matt. 11:23, Luke 12:47-48), there will be degrees of reward in heaven. In Luke 19:17-19 Jesus, in a parable, describes "good and faithful servants" who receive authority over either five or ten cities. The obvious interpretation is some get "more" in heaven than others. And "authority" over people and cities will be one of the primary rewards. Think of being mayor of New York City for 1000 years during the Millennium and welcomed into town by a ticker tape parade in your honor! And I think we can assume a similar realm of authority awaits many in the age beyond the millennium.

Please note, everybody is happy in heaven, but some will have unique rewards to enjoy throughout eternity. One such reward is where we get to live.

"In my Father's house are many mansions: if it were not so, I would have told you. I go to prepare a place for you" (John 14:1-2).

Notice two important things: Jesus said, "I go to prepare a place for you." If it only took Him six days to create the earth and all therein, think what He has prepared for us in 2000 years of creativity! Also notice Jesus mentions "My Father's house." God has a house! And in that house are "many mansions." In other translations, "dwellings" or "rooms." You will have your own place of reward. Just as today some have fabulous mansions in Beverly Hills and some humbler homes in the suburbs, where you live will be determined by HOW you now live!

"In the resurrection they neither marry, nor are given in marriage, but are as the angels of God in heaven" (Matt. 22:30).

No one is married in heaven (Sorry my Mormon friends!). For those who are very happily married, this may seem like a negative (To others, this may be what makes heaven, heaven!). But there will simply be no need for "mates" in heaven. We'll have no sexual desire:

"For all that is in the world, the lust of the flesh, and the lust of the eyes, and the pride of life, is not of the Father, but is of the world. And the world passes away, and the lust thereof: but he that does the will of God abides forever" (1 John 2:16-17 KJV).

No one is going to be asking, "Lord, I like it up here but I kind of miss sex. Anything you can do about that?" If the Lord created romantic love and sex in one day, I am sure in 2000 years he came up with many and even more enjoyable ways to find fun and personal fulfillment.

We likely will have our own favorite furnishings, musical instruments, sound systems, 3-D Holographic "TV's" where we can watch the heavenly news stations, maybe wonderful, (wholesome!) movies.

"For, behold, I create new heavens and a new earth" (Isa. 65:17).

The earth will be "new" and very different. For instance, there will be no oceans. (Rev. 21:1). The oceans are wonderful and beautiful, but we won't miss them! We likely will need all the land space for the animals as there is scriptural evidence for animals being in eternity (Rom. 8:20-21). The Lord may allow your favorite resurrected pets to live in your condo!

"And God shall wipe away all tears from their eyes; and there shall be no more death, neither

sorrow, nor crying, neither shall there be any more pain: for the former things are passed away" (Rev. 21:4).

Eternal life will be only wonderful with absolutely NO NEGATIVES! Revelation two and three list several "rewards" that await us in heaven:

"To him who overcomes I will give to eat from the tree of life" (Rev. 2:7 NKJV).

Enjoying food is one reward in heaven. Just as on earth the richer people get to eat in fancier restaurants with better surroundings and better quality food and poorer people have to eat at McDonalds (And the three dollar special at that!), I think it is reasonable to assume there will be better "restaurants" for some than others in heaven. So, from the Scriptures we can glean that our "rewards" in heaven will include such things as authority, bigger and better "rooms" than others, maybe better food and, simply put, more fun!

"He that overcomes, and keeps my works unto the end, to him will I give power over the nations" (Rev. 2:26 NKJV)

This could be referencing rewards for the 1000-year reign of Christ on earth. "Power over nations" obviously represents great authority. Wouldn't it be fun to be President of America! Of if you are a sports lover, manager of your favorite professional team? Some will be mayors of big cities and some of farming towns with 46 people. Your works on earth help determine which!

"He that overcomes will I make a pillar in the temple of my God, and he shall go no more out" (3:12).

A pillar is big, important, very conspicuous and virtually forever; fraught with meaning! I don't know for sure what "go no more out" means, but I think the closest thing may be what happened to me after a fabulous vacation with my entire family at Disneyworld in Florida in 2021. The last day, I dreaded going home because I was having such a wonderful, unforgettable time there. Such "farewells" or sad partings will never again happen as we "go no more out" (from Disneyworld …or God's protective, loving and kind presence!).

Finally, I find great motivation to be faithful to my personal call to follow the Lord in Eph. 2:7:

"That in the ages to come he might show the exceeding riches of his grace in his kindness toward us through Christ Jesus."

Notice it says, "ages to come." What new and thrilling "ages" await us?

Will God create new worlds with new beings for us to, like angels, oversee?

Will there be new, vast universes for us to explore?

God has created billions of stars, and millions of different species of flowers and animals on earth. Throughout eternity, His incredible imagination is going to bring everlasting joy, fascination, and ongoing and new rewards for the faithful.

Obey him, suffer for Him, overcome deadly sins and be faithful until the end and great will be your future rewards.

Heaven...it's a great place to spend eternity!

11

Satan's Lies About Hell

"The devil, who deceived them, was thrown into the fiery lake" (Rev. 20:10).

Satan, the John 8:44 "Father of lies," has convinced many people that Hell isn't really what we evangelical preachers say it is. Satan wants to convince mankind they don't have to worry about dying and going to Hell. Thus, he has concocted lies that, tragically, many believe. You can "believe a lie and be damned" (See 2 Thess. 2:8-12). Have you believed any of the following lies?

Satan's lie about Hell #1: "Hell is not hot!"

Some try to logically deduce God wouldn't send anybody to a terrible, hot, eternal punishment. But, if Hell weren't hot, why would our Lord and other biblical writers describe it repeatedly as a "fire?" Christ said, **"The Son... will cast them into the furnace of fire. There will be wailing and gnashing of teeth"** (Matt. 13:41, 42 NKJV).

Jesus called Hell a fire. If Hell were cold, wouldn't he have called it an "iceberg?" If it were entertainment, wouldn't He have called it a "theater?" No, He clearly describes it as a fire.

"If your hand or foot causes you to sin, cut it off and cast it from you. It is better for you to enter into life lame or maimed, rather than having two hands or two feet, to be cast into the everlasting fire" (Matt. 18:8 NKJV).

Above, Jesus calls Hell an "everlasting fire." If Hell weren't hot, wouldn't He sometimes have described it as something other than fire, perhaps an "everlasting wind" or an "everlasting river?" No, again, He clearly defines Hell as "fire." And fire is always hot! What part about "hot" don't people understand? If Jesus says Hell is hot, it must be hot, period! Those who believe "Hell is not hot" have simply rejected the clear revelation of God's Word and have accepted the devil's lie!

Lie #2: "Hell is not forever!"

(In other words, "you'll get a second chance.") False! Hell is eternal punishment, as Jesus said, **"And these will go away into everlasting punishment, but the righteous into eternal life"** (Matt. 25:46 NKJV). In the Bible, Hell, or future punishment, is often mentioned with the word "eternal" or "everlasting." That Hell is eternal is a truth accepted by the Church of Jesus Christ throughout its history. There is good reason, too; the scriptures clearly describe Hell as eternal. Yet, there are still some who teach or at least foster the hope there will be a second chance after death or after some short-term punishment.

Any false hope can be easily dismissed by biblical evidence! Jesus said,

"And if your foot causes you to sin, cut it off. It is better for you to enter life lame, rather than having two feet, to be cast into Hell, into the fire that shall never be quenched" (Matt. 26:24 NKJV).

Jesus didn't say, "Don't worry! The fires of Hell will burn out in a few millennia." No, he said, they "shall never be quenched." The word above, translated as "quenched," is the Greek word "asbestos." We use fibers called "asbestos," which in English means to make something "fireproof." The word in Greek means "unquenchable." In other words, Gehenna is a fire that can never be made fireproof, ever! It is unquenchable. It will never be put out. It is eternal punishment!

"The Lord Jesus is revealed from heaven with His mighty angels, in flaming fire taking vengeance on those who do not know God, and on those who do not obey the gospel of our Lord Jesus Christ. These shall be punished with everlasting destruction from the presence of the Lord and from the glory of His power" (2 Thess. 1:7-9 NKJV).

The "destruction" Hell produces is called "everlasting." He could have said "for a long, long time." He didn't. He said, "everlasting." Accept it. Believe it! There was once a commercial on TV advertising a pesticide (A box with a hole for cockroaches to crawl in to eat the food inside and get stuck). It was called the "Roach Motel." A spooky TV voice said, "They'll check in . . . but they won't check out!" Hell is like a "Roach motel."

Make your reservation for "Hotel Heaven" while you can still make a reservation! Don't take a chance with a "Roach Motel" like Hell! That Hell is eternal is indeed hard to understand this side of eternity. But, the Bible is very clear on the subject. And I trust the Bible. Do you? As the old gospel hymn says, "Farther along, we'll know all about it. Farther along, we'll understand why." Until then, let's just believe what the Bible says about Hell. It is eternal and there is no second chance to get out! Stay out of "Roach Motels" and stay out of Hell! You can be sure of one thing about Hell: you'll get in...but you won't get out!"

Lie #3: "Hell is just the grave!"

We know this is not true because the scriptures make plain the soul is immortal and indestructible. It doesn't cease to exist at death. The soul goes somewhere...

"Judas by transgression fell, that he might go to his own place" (Acts 1:25 NKJV).

Judas, Christ's betrayer, had "his own place" of punishment awaiting him. All sinners have a future location where they experience their "own place" of punishment.

When Jesus spoke of Gehenna, the Lake of fire, He said:

"If your hand causes you to sin, cut it off. It is better for you to enter into life maimed, rather than having two hands, to go to Hell, into the fire that shall never be quenched" (Mark 9:43 NKJV).

What possible difference would it make to a sinner if the fire never goes out if he is only relegated to a cold grave? Jesus continued in verse 44: **"Their worm does not die And the fire is not quenched."**

It says the "worm does not die." The people around Jerusalem could certainly understand that phrase concerning Hell. In the Gehenna "dump" outside of Jerusalem, maggots could be seen eating at the corpses of dead animal bodies that the flames had not completely consumed. Why would Jesus refer to the "worm?" Maggots (The larvae of flies that lay their eggs on corpses) symbolize death, and they are disgusting and ugly. But, Jesus' emphasis was less on the maggot itself and rather on the fact the "worm does not die." Maggots forever digging and eating: this alludes to a punishment that never ends and does not cease at death!

Then, when Jesus added, "the fire is not quenched," the residents of Jerusalem could also readily visualize that analogy. The fires of the Gehenna "dump" smoldered continually for many years. If Jesus had wanted to communicate Gehenna as a place of perpetual unconsciousness and annihilation, He could have referred to the local graveyard or pointed to a coffin or a sepulcher, explaining, "See that coffin. See that still dead body. That is your future in Gehenna!" But, He didn't! Instead, He referred to Gehenna: a place of perpetual fire, worms, and smoke! There must have been a reason for this: He wanted to communicate as clearly and accurately as possible the truth of eternal punishment to their contemporary minds.

There should be no surprises in eternity for either believers or unbelievers if they will but study and believe the Bible. Hell is NOT just the grave! It's a place of literal, eternal punishment beyond the grave.

Lie #4: Hell is the same punishment for all!

"And I saw the dead, small and great, standing before God, and books were opened. And another book was opened, which is the Book of Life. And the dead were judged according to their works, by the things which were written in the books" (Rev. 20:12).

"For we must all appear before the judgment seat of Christ; that every one may receive the things done in his body, according to that he hath done, whether it be good or bad" (2 Cor. 5:10 NKJV).

The coming judgments for works determine the kinds of rewards the believer receives in Heaven and what punishments the unbeliever receives in Hell. Jesus said,

"And you, Capernaum, who are exalted to heaven, will be brought down to Hades; for if the mighty works which were done in you had been done in Sodom, it would have remained until this day...it shall be more tolerable for the land of Sodom in the Day of Judgment than for you" (Matt. 11:23, 24 NKJV).

Punishment will be "more tolerable" for some than for others. This truth should put the fear of God in all because of sins we so flippantly commit. In God's eyes, it is possible our little sin (because of our greater knowledge) is more serious to Him than the big sin that caused Him to destroy Sodom and Gomorrah! And, in view of this, what punishment are we likely bringing upon "Christian" America for our flagrant sins when we have so many things to enlighten us against the sin: churches on every other corner, Christian television, Christian radio, YouTube teachings, Christian books sold in many stores, and Bibles gathering dust on our shelves!

How "tolerable" will Hell be for a sinner? Again, that is determined by his works while on Earth.

"But in accordance with your hardness and your impenitent heart you are treasuring up for yourself

wrath in the day of wrath and revelation of the righteous judgment of God" (Romans 2:5 NKJV).

Like a man saving money in a piggy bank, many are "treasuring up" for themselves an increasingly growing measure of "wrath" which awaits them on the "day of wrath." Avoid God's wrath!

Lie #5, "A Loving God wouldn't send anybody to Hell!"

There is a theological viewpoint referred to as: "universal reconciliation," "universalism," or "ultimate reconciliation." The reasoning goes like this: God is a God of love; Eternal punishment in Hell is not an expression of love; Therefore, either there is no Hell, or if there is a Hell, ultimately, God will save everybody from it. This is a pleasant thought. There is only one problem: it is fully contradicted by the Word of God. "A loving God wouldn't send anybody to Hell!" is one of the most common things I hear unbelievers say when I mention Hell. My answer is:

"God doesn't send you to Hell. You send yourself!"

How could a loving God send anyone to Hell? Well, every day, kind, considerate, "loving" just judges with wives and children, dole out 150-year sentences or even the death penalty to men who break the laws of man. God also is a just judge who has a "loving" family. Although He loves the sinner and His Son died to save sinners from

Hell, in His justice, God still must sentence them to 150 trillion years in Hell.

A robber can make a split decision and pull a trigger killing someone in less than one second. Yet, for that crime, a judge may sentence him to over a billion seconds in prison! If this is true of "loving judges" on earth, then why would it seem so incongruous that a "loving God" would sentence a sinner who sinned for 80 years on earth to Hell for a similarly proportionate 80 billion years of punishment?

People always say, **"God is a God of love."** (And He is). But, if they would read their Bible, they would see He also is a God of, **"terror"** (II Cor. 5:11), a **"consuming fire"** (Heb. 12:29), **a "jealous God"** (Deut. 6:15), **"angry with the wicked every day"** (Psalm 7:11), **"the judge"** (Ps. 75:7), and is the one who created Hell in the first place (Matt. 25:41).

Today, America's moral values are greatly flawed. Whether values come from a Supreme Court judge, scientist, philosopher, theologian, or a high-school dropout, we cannot trust our human ideas about right and wrong. That is why God gave us the Bible. That is why Jesus preached more about Hell than He did about the love of God. Jesus is the one, more than anyone in the Bible, who gave us the most descriptive picture of Hell as a terrible place of eternal punishment.

If you have made Satan's lie and the overused "religious" cliché, "A loving God wouldn't send anyone to Hell," your excuse for sin, you have rejected the revelation of God's Word. And, you are guilty of violating Jesus' warning,

"...to everyone who hears the words of the prophecy of this book: If anyone adds to these things, God will add to him the plagues that are written in this book...if anyone takes away from the words of the book of this prophecy, God shall take away his part from the Book of Life, from the holy city" (Rev. 22:18 NKJV).

Revelation teaches clearly about the fires of Hell. Anyone who rejects the teaching of that book or "takes away from the words of the book" will forfeit Heaven and end up in the very Hell he thinks God wouldn't send anyone to. Surely this would be the greatest irony ever! Don't be guilty of it.

Some closing lessons from the Word of God...

"And if your eye causes you to sin, pluck it out and cast it from you. It is better for you to enter into life with one eye, rather than having two eyes, to be cast into Hell (Gehenna) **fire"** (Matt 18:9 NKJV). Jesus said this. Visualize the pain and horror of ripping an eye out of its socket and spending a lifetime wearing an eye patch to cover a bloody, painful, sunken hole in the head!

Satan's Lies About Hell

Yet, Jesus said this would be preferred to the Hellfire to come. The scriptures above are why I started praying many years ago,

"Lord, if you see I'm about to backslide and end up in Hell, kill me first!"

A sobering warning to all is given in Hebrews 10:31:

"Falling into the hands of the living God is a terrifying thing."

What "terrifying thing" awaits those unprepared to meet their Creator and Judge in the world to come? Is the word "terrifying" symbolic? Symbolic of what? If God didn't mean what He said, why didn't He say what He meant? If Hell is less horrible than the Bible describes, fine. But I wouldn't count on it! The only thing we can ever really count on in life is the Bible and Jesus, and they are both very clear about Hell. If you have not done what is necessary to escape this future horrible eternal punishment, be sure to read the last chapter of the book in your hands!

To all who are escaping eternal judgment, I'll see you in the other place! Jesus is waiting to greet us with His outstretched nail-scarred hands. Let His Hands pull you forever from the eternal fiery pit below! Read how next...

12

The Way Out

"You were to them God-Who-Forgives, Though you took vengeance on their deeds" (Ps. 99:8 NKJV).

We saw in the last chapter that God will take "vengeance" on the "deeds" of those who are unprepared to face Him at the judgment. That's the bad news. But the good news is God is still a God of love. He is identified as the "God-Who-Forgives." His loving heart is ready to forgive every sin! But there is only one way to discover that forgiveness and that "way" is to, **"Follow the way of love"** (1 Cor. 14:1 NIV).

Are you following that way? You think so? But are you SURE? God gave us the Son of God and the Word of God so we could be absolutely certain about our eternal destiny:

"He who has the Son has life; he who does not have the Son of God does not have life. These things I have written to you who believe in the name of the Son of God, that you may know that you have eternal life" (1 John 5:12, 13).

Let me help you make your own determination by first asking you some questions. Don't take a chance on making the biggest mistake of your life! First,

"Where and when were you born?" (The city and date). You surely know where and when you were born on planet Earth. Now, here is an even more important question: Where and when were you born again? This is paramount because Jesus said, **"Very truly I tell you, no one can see the kingdom of God unless they are born again"** (John 3:3 NIV).

What would your answer be to the question, "Where and when were you born again?" Perhaps you would say...

"I was born again when I was baptized." (As you'll read below, that is NOT how we are born again)

"I was born again when I joined my church." (Not a bad idea, but that does not make you born-again)

"I was born again when I invited Christ into my life many years ago." (That's a wonderful thing to do for sure, but is Christ in your life NOW?).

We are discussing your eternal destiny, so, for your own welfare, finish reading this chapter before you put away this book!

How do you know if you were born again? The Bible must be your determinate factor: **"The words that I have spoken to you will be your judge in that day"** (John 12:48 NKJV).

If you know where and when you were born, but aren't 100% sure you were ever born again, let Christ's words and the Bible show you how.

Being born again is like the birth of a baby: one day, in a dark womb, the next day, living in the light! **"He has called you out of darkness and into His marvelous light"** (Romans 3:23 NKJV). God is urging you to escape what Christ called "outer darkness" and to come to the light, **"The words that I speak to you are...life"** (John 6:63 NKJV). Concerning this "life," there is a book in heaven called the Book of Life.

On the judgment day, when you stand before God, that book will be opened to see if your name is in it. **"Whoever was not written in the Book of Life was cast into the lake of fire"** (Rev. 20:15 NKJV). A newborn is given a birth-certificate which contains their name. Similarly, if you are born again, your name is written in the Book of Life.

Consider what is at stake here! Either Hell or heaven is everyone's destiny. Becoming a born-again Christian is the ONLY WAY to avoid Hell and experience eternal light and eternal life. So, is your name written in the Book of Life? If you are in doubt, become a born-again Christian.

How then is a person born again? First, you must repent of your sins. Jesus said, **"Unless you repent you will ...perish"** (Luke 13:3). Repent means to turn away from any habitual, chronic, willful sins and to dedicate yourself to overcoming such sins and bringing your life in line with Christ's teachings in the Bible. You will be judged, not by what your church or my church might believe. We both will be judged by the Bible!

Perhaps you think you're already good enough in God's eyes to make heaven? Think again! **"There is no one who does good, no, not one"** (Romans 3:12). God's Word says you're a sinner, **"All have sinned and fall short of the glory (presence) of God"** (Romans 3:23). Thus, you cannot "earn" the privilege of living in His eternal presence. **"He saved us, not because we did the right things, but...by a new birth"** (Titus 3:5). See the way to be saved (from Hell)? It's "by the new birth."

Do you think that you have a good heart? Think again! **"The heart is deceitful above all things and desperately wicked"** (Jer. 17:9). Your heart may seem okay in your mind, but God sees a lifetime of anger, pride, hatred, jealousy, or lust; and all these are "desperately wicked" to Him! Because of these sins, you'll one day face a payday. **"The wages of sin** is (eternal) **death"** (Romans 6:23 NKJV).

Not only you and I, but God said, **"the entire world is guilty before God"** (Romans 3:19 NLT). You may not be guilty of murder, but are you guilty of lying? **"all liars shall have their part in the lake which burns with fire"** (Rev. 21:8). You may not be guilty of stealing, but are you guilty of sexual sin? **"whoever looks with lust at a woman has already committed adultery in his heart"** (Matt. 5:28).

You may have kept God's laws many times in your life, but all the good deeds you have done in the past can never compensate, in God's eyes, for your past sins. Imagine a murderer, found guilty, standing in court. The judge asks him, "Do you have anything to say before I pronounce your sentence?" To which the defendant says, "All my life I did a lot of good things: paid my taxes, was a Boy Scout leader, food-bank volunteer, and obeyed all the other laws. So, couldn't you, on that basis, set me free?" Of course not! A just judge would still commit the criminal to prison.

Similarly, no matter how well you might have obeyed God's laws, that is not enough in God's eyes to get you into heaven. **"No one is made right with God by obeying the law"** (Gal. 2:16 NIRV). You need a Savior. He is ready to save you, but you must follow His way.

"I am the way, the truth, and the life. No man comes to the Father except by me" (John 14:6). **"Salvation comes no other way; no other name** (but Jesus) **has been or will be given to us by which we can be saved, only this one"** (Acts 4:12 MSG).

Jesus gives you this personal invitation. He said, **"Come to me"** (Matt. 11:28). Will you "come" to Him today? Again, Jesus said you must "repent." Will you repent?

Repentance requires two steps as Prov. 28:13 (NKJV) explains, **"He who covers his sins will not prosper, But whoever confesses and forsakes them will have mercy."**

First, "confess" you are a sinner and ask the Lord to forgive you. Then, "forsake" your sins. Your conscience will reveal things you need to stop doing, places you need to stop going, and words you need to stop saying. God will help you do this when you invite Him into your life (You have not been able to do it on your own, anyway, have you?).

Humbly ask Him to save you, **"Everyone who calls on the name of the Lord will be saved"** (Romans 10:13). If you were swimming in the ocean and a riptide began pulling you out to sea and, exhausted, you began to drown, but suddenly saw a lifeguard walking on the shore, what would you say to the lifeguard?

You'd cry, "I'm drowning. Save me!" All sinners are drowning in sin, but Jesus is ready to hear their prayers for help and save them from sinking into Hell.

Maybe you once were a true Christian. You accepted Christ, attended church, studied the Bible, and strived to live the right life. But a bad church experience, a hurtful personal relationship, or a great temptation caused you to drift away from the Lord. As you read this, if you were to suddenly die of a heart attack, do you fear you might go to Hell? Don't gamble with your soul! Why? If you once knew the right way, but turned away from it, you'll have a worse punishment in Hell than ever. **"And a servant who knows what the master wants, but isn't prepared and doesn't carry out those instructions, will be severely punished"** (Luke 12:47 NLT).

Even if your name was at one time written in the Book of Life, it can be "blotted out" by sin: **"Whoever has sinned against me I will blot out of my book.** (Ex. 32:33 NIV). So, whether your name was ever in the book, or not, add your name to it today!

Here is Christ's personal invitation to all,

"Behold, I stand at the door and knock. If anyone hears My voice and opens the door, I will come in to him" (Rev. 3:20).

Jesus is knocking at the door of your heart. He wants to come into your life. He wants to forgive you of every sin you have ever committed. He wants to make you a born-again Christian. He wants to write your name in the Book of Life. So, will you choose heaven over Hell today? Will you "come" to the only way out of Hell to get on the path toward Heaven? Will you confess your sins, repent of them, and begin following Christ today, and for the rest of your life? If so, here is a prayer proven to pave the way for millions to gain eternal life. Pray it out loud to the Lord now, if you can sincerely mean it:

"Dear Father in heaven. I admit I am a sinner. I repent of my sins. Please forgive me. I invite Jesus to come into my heart. Make me a born again Christian. Write my name in the Book of Life, so I can go to heaven instead of Hell. I'll follow Jesus, I'll obey Your Word, fight sin, and fight Satan. And by the grace of God, I'll live for You, for the rest of my life. So, help me God."

If you prayed that prayer and meant it, you are now saved, according to God's promises. You may feel the same as you did a moment ago, but the Christian life is a life of faith. **"By grace are you saved through faith"** (Eph. 2:8). You believe, but now, because you have chosen to believe in God's Word, you are called to follow His instructions for your life. **"blessed are all who hear the word of God and put it into practice"** (Luke 11:28). Start "practicing" being a follower of Christ.

Here's a first Word of God rule to follow: **"If you openly declare that Jesus is Lord and believe in your heart that God raised him from the dead, you will be saved."** (Romans 10:9 NLT). Go tell someone you know, maybe even a person who gave you this book, that you are now a born-again Christian!

Then, your next rule to follow is to be baptized in water. Jesus said, **"Whoever believes and is baptized will be saved"** (Mark 16:16). This is your first step of obedience to the Lord. Baptism is another way we "openly declare" Jesus is our Lord. Baptism, by full immersion, not sprinkling, is the way the rite, ceremony, or observance should be performed. The very word "baptism" in the original biblical language (Greek) means "to be totally immersed in water." And that is how Jesus' disciples baptized and how John the Baptizer baptized.

If you were sprinkled as a child, that wasn't a bad thing, but it wasn't true baptism and it would not count in God's eyes as a biblical act of obedience. Notice above Jesus said, "He who believes" (an infant can't believe yet!).

Furthermore, Acts 2:38 says, **"Repent and be baptized."** An intelligent decision to turn away from our sins is FIRST required before being baptized. So, if you believe, and if you repent, you can and should now be baptized. Call a pastor and ask him when he could baptize you. Christianity is not a personal, private, quiet religion you live at home. By publically being baptized, you bear witness to family, friends, and the world you are a follower of Christ, your Savior. The best place to be baptized is at a church, or at least with a church congregation, at a pool, lake, or beach. It is a perfect time to invite those you care about to witness your decision. After all, if you aren't going to Hell now, you certainly want them to join you on "The Way Out," don't you? Set the example!

Church should now be a top priority in your life. Church is not a building, though we call buildings with a cross on them, "churches." However, the church, in God's eyes, is comprised of all His true followers who gather to gather to worship and learn more about Him, on the local level.

"For where two or three gather together as my followers, I am there among them" (NLT).

"Where" could include just a handful or so gathering together in a living room to "meet" with Jesus. But, regardless of where, know for sure: Jesus goes to "church" every Sunday! If you are going to "follow" Him, you need to follow Him there.

Join a group of fellow believers at a church as soon as possible. Ask God to guide you to a good church near you. Call a Christian friend and ask for their recommendation. Don't just go back to the church you may have been raised in. If the teachings of that church did not lead you to Christ (and you needed this book to make up for that lack), then that is a sign you would be better off visiting another church.

It is a mistake to try to be a Christian without going to church. You need the Bible teachings. You need to develop helpful, supportive relationships with others also sincerely following the "way." In the last days, it will be a serious mistake to not regularly attend church: "

And let us not neglect our meeting together, as some people do, but encourage one another, especially now that the day of his return is drawing near" (Heb.10:25 NLT).

Read and study the Bible daily. If you only have an old King James Version Bible, written using many no longer used English words, buy a modern translation. For example, the NIV, GW, NKJV, and NLT are versions used often in this book. Begin in the New Testament at first (Start with John). It was reading the Bible every day, searching for truth that convinced me to become a born-again Christian when I was a confused teenager (Read the whole story in my autobiography, *EVANGELIST: MY LIFE STORY; MY LIFE JOURNEY*).

Begin and end your days with prayer. Ask God for guidance, protection, and wisdom to make the right decisions. Ask Him for His strength to overcome temptation. If you should fail and sin (and you will, for we all do!), He doesn't immediately blot your name from the

Book of Life. Remember, He is the "God-Who-Forgives." Kneel in humble repentance and confess your sin to Him (not to a man!):

"If we confess our sins, He is faithful and just to forgive us our sins and to cleanse us from all unrighteousness" (1 John 1:9 NKJV).

You may not feel better immediately, but that is where faith comes in. He is faithful (to His promises), and if you confess the sin, He will forgive you. Period! And once your sin is forgiven, He also forgets you even did it!

"I will be merciful to their unrighteousness, and their sins... I will remember no more" (Heb. 8:12 NKJV).

Put your sins behind you! God forgets your sins, you can too!

One final thing. As you now are endeavoring to "follow the way of love," a foremost responsibility in your life is to love the world as Christ did. He died a cruel death so men might be saved. Will you love the world so much you will now die to your pride, selfishness, or fear? Will you spread the message about the love that can save everyone from an eternal Hell?

Here is Christ's clear command for you, me, and all born-again Christians:

"Go everywhere and announce the Message of God's good news to one and all" (Mark 16:15).

Spread the message.

Phone, text, email, write, or visit someone today.

Perhaps buy them one of these books or at least share your copy with them.

Warn them!

Show them "The Way Out."

Help prepare them by telling them what you have learned...

About the Future

(Turn to the next page for more helpful information)

To receive Dea's free daily email teachings, go to his website: deawarford.org. You may also order his books from the website, or through Amazon.com or Barnes & Noble.

Other Book titles by Evangelist Dea Warford

EVANGELIST: MY LIFE STORY; MY LIFE JOURNEY

MIRACLES ARE YOUR DESTINY

Dea is ready to answer your questions at his email address:

evangelist@deawarford.org

About the Future

...may be purchased in bulk wholesale prices for distribution to both individuals and churches by ordering them by email at the above address...

Made in the USA
Columbia, SC
30 May 2023

17401888R00063